Climate Change: The EU Emissions Trading Scheme (ETS) Gets Ready for Kyoto

Larry Parker

The BiblioGov Project is an effort to expand awareness of the public documents and records of the U.S. Government via print publications. In broadening the public understanding of government and its work, an enlightened democracy can grow and prosper. Ranging from historic Congressional Bills to the most recent Budget of the United States Government, the BiblioGov Project spans a wealth of government information. These works are now made available through an environmentally friendly, print-on-demand basis, using only what is necessary to meet the required demands of an interested public. We invite you to learn of the records of the U.S. Government, heightening the knowledge and debate that can lead from such publications.

Included are the following Collections:

Budget of The United States Government
Presidential Documents
United States Code
Education Reports from ERIC
GAO Reports
History of Bills
House Rules and Manual
Public and Private Laws

Code of Federal Regulations
Congressional Documents
Economic Indicators
Federal Register
Government Manuals
House Journal
Privacy act Issuances
Statutes at Large

Order Code RL34150

CRS Report for Congress

Climate Change: The EU Emissions Trading Scheme (ETS) Enters Kyoto Compliance Phase

Updated February 11, 2008

Larry Parker
Specialist in Energy and Environmental Policy
Resources, Science, and Industry Division

Congressional
Research
Service

Prepared for Members and
Committees of Congress

Climate Change: The EU Emissions Trading Scheme (ETS) Enters Kyoto Compliance Phase

Summary

The European Union's (EU) Emissions Trading Scheme (ETS) is a cornerstone of the EU's efforts to meet its obligation under the Kyoto Protocol. It covers more than 11,500 energy intensive facilities across the 27 EU Member countries; covered entities emit about 45% of the EU's carbon dioxide emissions. A "Phase 1" trading period began January 1, 2005. A second, Phase 2, trading period began in 2008, covering the period of the Kyoto Protocol, with a third one planned for 2013.

Several positives resulting from the Phase 1 "learning by doing" exercise may assist the ETS in making the Phase 2 process run more smoothly, including: (1) greatly improving emissions data, (2) encouraging development of the Kyoto Protocol's project-based mechanisms — Clean Development Mechanism (CDM) and Joint Implementation (JI), and (3) influencing corporate behavior to begin pricing in the value of allowances in decision-making, particularly in the electric utility sector.

However, several issues that arose during the first phase remain contentious as the ETS moves into Phase 2, including allocation schemes, shutdown credits and new entrant reserves, and others. In addition, the expansion of the EU and the implementation of the directives linking the ETS to the Kyoto Protocol project-based mechanisms created new issues to which Phase 2 has had to respond.

The United States is not a party to Kyoto. However, almost three years of carbon emissions trading has given the EU valuable experience as it prepares for Kyoto. This experience, along with the process of developing Phase 2 NAPs, may provide some insight into cap-and-trade design issues currently being debated in the U.S.

- The U.S. currently requires only electric utilities to monitor CO_2. The EU-ETS experience suggests expanding similar requirements to all facilities covered under a cap-and-trade scheme would be pivotal for developing allocation systems, reduction targets, and enforcement provisions.
- In the U.S. debate on comprehensive versus sector-specific reduction programs, the EU-ETS experience suggests that adding sectors to a trading scheme once established may be a slow, contentious process.
- As with most EU industries, most U.S. industry groups either oppose auctions outright or want them to be supplemental to a base free allocation. The EU-ETS experience suggests Congress may want to consider specifying any auction requirement if it wishes to incorporate market economics more fully into compliance decisions.
- EU-ETS analysis suggests the most important variables in determining Phase 1 allowance price changes were oil and natural gas price changes; an apparent linkage that raises possible market manipulation issues, particularly with the inclusion of financial instruments such as options and futures contracts. Congress may consider whether the Securities and Exchange Commission or the Commodities Futures Trading Commission should have regulatory and oversight authority over such instruments.

Contents

Overview 1

National Allocation Plans and the ETS 3
    Need for Further Emissions Reductions 5
    Need to Adjust ETS Allocations 8

Issues Arising in NAPs for the ETS 10
    Supplementarity 10
    Auction Policy 13
    New Entrant Reserves 15
    Closure Policy 17
    Benchmarking 18
    Allocation and Energy Policy 19
    Expansion 22
    Harmonization 22

Summary and Considerations for U.S. Cap-and-Trade Proposals 23
    Emission Inventories and Target Setting 23
    Coverage 24
    Allocation Schemes 25
    Flexibility and Price Volatility 26

List of Figures

Figure 1. ECX CFI Futures Contracts: Price and Volume 7
Figure 2. Actual and Projected Emissions for EU-25 and EU-15 9

List of Tables

Table 1. ETS Annual Allocations for Phase 2: 2008-2012 4
Table 2. JI/CDM Limits for Phase 2: 2008-2012 11
Table 3. Value of Annual Allocation for New NGCC Powerplant 17

Climate Change: The EU Emissions Trading Scheme (ETS) Enters Kyoto Compliance Phase

Overview

Climate change is generally viewed as a global issue, but proposed responses typically require action at the national level. With the 1997 Kyoto Protocol now in force and setting emissions objectives for 2008-2012, countries that ratified the protocol are developing appropriate implementation strategies to begin reducing their emissions of greenhouse gases.[1] In particular, the European Union (EU) has decided to use an emissions trading scheme (called a "cap-and-trade" program), along with other market-oriented mechanisms permitted under the Protocol, to help it achieve compliance at least cost.[2] The decision to use emission trading to implement the Kyoto Protocol is at least partly based on the successful emissions trading program used by the United States to implement its sulfur dioxide (acid rain) control program contained in Title IV of the 1990 Clean Act Amendments.[3]

The EU's Emissions Trading System (ETS) covers more than 11,500 energy intensive facilities across the 27 EU Member countries, including oil refineries, powerplants over 20 megawatts (MW) in capacity, coke ovens, and iron and steel plants, along with cement, glass, lime, brick, ceramics, and pulp and paper installations. Covered entities emit about 45% of the EU's carbon dioxide emissions. The trading program covers neither CO_2 emissions from the transportation sector, which account for about 25% of the EU's total greenhouse gas emissions, nor emissions of non-CO_2 greenhouse gases, which account for about 20% of the EU's total greenhouse gas emissions. A "Phase 1" trading period began January 1, 2005.[4]

---

[1] Six gases are included under the Kyoto Protocol: carbon dioxide, methane, nitrous oxide, hydrofluorocarbons, perfluorocarbons, and sulfur hexafluoride. The United States has not ratified the Kyoto Protocol and, therefore, is not covered by its provisions. For more information on the Kyoto Protocol, see CRS Report RL33826, *Climate Change: The Kyoto Protocol and International Actions,* by Susan Fletcher and Larry Parker.

[2] Norway, a non-EU country, also has instituted a CO_2 trading system. Various other countries and a state-sponsored regional initiative located in the northeastern United States involving several states are developing mandatory cap-and-trade system programs, but are not operating at the current time. For a review of these emerging programs, along with other voluntary efforts, see International Energy Agency, *Act Locally, Trade Globally* (2005).

[3] P.L. 101-549, Title IV (November 15, 1990).

[4] For further background on the ETS and its first year of operation, see CRS Report RL33581, *Climate Change: The European Union's Emissions Trading System (EU-ETS),*

(continued...)

A second, Phase 2, trading period began January 1, 2008, covering the period of the Kyoto Protocol, with a third one planned to begin in 2013.[5]

Under the Kyoto Protocol, the then-existing 15 nations of the EU agreed to reduce their aggregate annual average emissions for 2008-2012 by 8% from 1990 levels under a collective arrangement called a "bubble." By 2001, collective greenhouse gas emissions in the EU were 2.3% below 1990 levels, mostly the result of a structural shift from coal to natural gas in the United Kingdom and the incorporation of East Germany into West Germany. Several countries, including Ireland, Spain, and Portugal, experienced emissions growth of over 30% during this period.[6] In light of the Kyoto Protocol targets, the EU adopted a directive establishing the EU-ETS that entered into force October 13, 2003.[7] The importance of emissions trading was elevated by the accession of 10 additional central and eastern Europe countries to EU membership in May 2004. Collectively, these 10 countries' greenhouse gas emissions dropped 22.6% from 1990-2001, with only Slovenia's emissions increasing during that time (10.4%). With the accession of Bulgaria and Romania in January 2007, this expansion of the EU trading zone to 27 countries greatly increases the opportunities for cost-effective allowance trades.

The EC hopes that the Phase 1 "learning by doing" exercise has prepared the community for the more difficult task of achieving the reduction requirements of the Kyoto Protocol. Several positives have resulted from the Phase 1 experience that will assist the ETS in making the Phase 2 process run smoothly. First, Phase 1 established much of the critical infrastructure necessary for a functional emission market, including emissions monitoring, registries, and inventories. Much of the publicized difficulties the ETS experienced in the first phase can be traced to inadequate emission data.[8] Phase 1 has significantly improved those data in preparation for Phase 2.

---

[4] (...continued)
by Larry Parker.

[5] More information, including relevant directives, on the EU-ETS is available on the European Union's website at [http://europa.eu.int/scadplus/leg/en/lvb/l28012.htm].

[6] Pew Center on Global Climate Change, *The European Union Emissions Trading Scheme (EU-ETS): Insights and Opportunities* (no date), available at [http://www.pewclimate.org/docUploads/EU%2DETS%20White%20Paper%2Epdf].

[7] Directive 2003/87/EC of the European Parliament and of the Council of 13 October 2003 establishing a scheme for greenhouse gas emissions allowance trading within the Community and amending Council Directive 96/61/EC.

[8] A Denny Ellerman and Barbara K. Buchner, "The European Union Emissions Trading Scheme: Origins, Allocations, and Early Results," 1 *Environmental Economics and Policy* 1 (Winter 2007), pp. 69-70; and, International Emissions Trading Association, "IETA Position Paper on EU ETS Marking Functioning," (no date), p. 3.

Second, the ETS has helped jump-start the project-based mechanisms — Clean Development Mechanism (CDM) and Joint Implementation (JI) — created under the Kyoto Protocol.[9] As stated by Ellerman and Buchner:

> The access to external credits provided by the Linking Directive has had an invigorating effect on the CDM and more generally on CO_2 reduction projects in developing countries, especially in China and India, the two major countries that will eventually have to become part of a global climate regime if there is to be one.[10]

Third, according to the EC, a key result of Phase 1 has been its effect on corporate behavior. An EC survey of stakeholders indicates that many participants are pricing in the value of allowances in making decisions, particularly in the electric utility sector where 70% of firms stated they were pricing in the value of allowances into their daily operations, and 87% into future marginal pricing decisions. All industries state that it was a factor in long-term decision-making.[11]

However, several issues that arose during the first phase remain contentious as the ETS moves into Phase 2, including allocation (including use of auctions and reliance on model projections), shutdown credits and new entrant reserves, and others. In addition, the expansion of the EU and the implementation of the linking directives create new issues to which Phase 2 has had to respond. These new and continuing challenges, and the ETS response to them are discussed below.

National Allocation Plans and the ETS

National Allocation Plans (NAPs) are central to the EU's effort to achieve its Kyoto obligations. Each Member of the EU must submit a NAP that lays out its allocation scheme under the ETS, including individual allocations to each affected unit. For the second trading period, these NAPs were assessed by the EC to determine compliance with 12 criteria delineated in an annex to the emissions trading directive.[12] Criteria include requirements that the emissions caps and other measures

---

[9] For more on the effect of the ETS on Kyoto mechanisms, see A Denny Ellerman and Barbara K. Buchner, "The European Union Emissions Trading Scheme: Origins, Allocations, and Early Results," 1 *Environmental Economics and Policy* 1 (Winter 2007), p. 84; and, International Emissions Trading Association, "IETA Position Paper on EU ETS Market Functioning," (no date), p. 2. For more information on the Kyoto Protocol mechanisms, see CRS Report RL33826, *Climate Change: The Kyoto Protocol and International Actions*, by Susan Fletcher and Larry Parker.

[10] A Denny Ellerman and Barbara K. Buchner, "The European Union Emissions Trading Scheme: Origins, Allocations, and Early Results," 1 *Environmental Economics and Policy* 1 (Winter 2007), p. 84.

[11] European Commission, Directorate General for Environment, *Review of EU Emissions Trading Scheme: Survey Highlights*, (November 2005), pp. 5-7.

[12] Commission of the European Communities, Directive 2003/87/EC, available at [http://eur-lex.europa.eu/LexUriServ/LexUriServ.do?uri=OJ:L:2003:275:0032:0046:EN:

proposed by the Member State are sufficient to put it on the path toward its Kyoto target, protections against discrimination between companies and sectors, delineation of intended use of CDM and JI credits for compliance, along with provisions for new entrants, clean technology, and early reduction credits. For the second trading period, the NAP must guarantee Kyoto compliance.

NAPs for the second trading period were due June 30, 2006. As of October 26, 2007, the EC had reviewed and approved (sometimes conditionally) all 27 Member States' NAPs. As indicated by **Table 1**, the EC has reduced the proposed allocations of individual Member States by an average of 10.5% to increase the probability that the EU will achieve its target under the Kyoto Protocol. The need to reduce the requested allocations reflects both the structure of the ETS and the lessons the EC learned during the first phase.

Table 1. ETS Annual Allocations for Phase 2: 2008-2012

Member State	2005 Emissions (MMTCO$_2$E)	Proposed Kyoto Cap (MMTCO$_2$E)	EC Approved Kyoto Cap (MMTCO$_2$E)	Approved as Percent of Proposed
Austria	33.4	32.8	30.7	93.6%
Belgium	55.4	63.3	58.5	92.4%
Bulgaria	40.6	67.6	42.3	62.6%
Czech Rep.	82.5	101.9	86.8	85.2%
Cyprus	5.1	7.12	5.48	77%
Denmark	26.5	24.5	24.5	100%
Estonia	12.62	24.38	12.72	52.2%
Finland	33.1	39.6	37.6	94.8%
France	131.3	132.8	132.8	100%
Germany	474	482	453.1	94%
Greece	71.3	75.5	69.1	91.5%
Hungary	26.0	30.7	26.9	87.6%
Ireland	22.4	22.6	22.3	98.6%
Italy	225.5	209	195.8	93.7%
Latvia	2.9	7.7	3.43	44.5%
Lithuania	6.6	16.6	8.8	53%

[12] (...continued)
PDF].

Member State	2005 Emissions (MMTCO$_2$E)	Proposed Kyoto Cap (MMTCO$_2$E)	EC Approved Kyoto Cap (MMTCO$_2$E)	Approved as Percent of Proposed
Luxembourg	2.6	3.95	2.5	63%
Malta	1.98	2.96	2.1	71%
Netherlands	80.35	90.4	85.8	94.9%
Poland	203.1	284.6	208.5	73.3%
Portugal	36.4	35.9	34.8	96.9%
Romania	70.8	95.7	75.9	79.3%
Slovakia	25.2	41.3	30.9	74.8%
Slovenia	8.7	8.3	8.3	100%
Spain	182.6	152.7	152.3	99.7%
Sweden	19.3	25.2	22.8	90.5%
UK	242.4	246.2	246.2	100%
Total	2122.16	2325.34	2080.93	89.5%

Source: European Commission, "Emissions Trading: EU-wide cap for 2008-2012 set at 2.08 billion allowances after assessment of national plans for Bulgaria," EC Press Release, October 26, 2007.

Need for Further Emissions Reductions

It is unclear to what degree the first phase of the ETS achieved real emissions reductions. Emissions are dynamic over time; a product of a country's population, economic activity, and greenhouse gas intensity.[13] To capture these dynamics, the Member States of the EU develop emissions baselines from models that project future trends in a country's emissions based on these and other factors, such as anticipated energy and greenhouse gas policies.[14] During the first phase, the emissions goal was to put the EU on the path to Kyoto compliance — not actually comply with the Protocol (which wasn't necessary until the 2008-2012 time period). Thus, countries developed "business as usual" baselines based on projected growth in emissions. Such a projected baseline suffers from two sources of uncertainty: data uncertainties, and forecasting uncertainties. On data, Phase 1 suffered from uncertainties with respect to data collection and coverage, in monitoring methods for

---

[13] For more information, see CRS Report RL33970, *Greenhouse Gas Emission Drivers: Population, Economic Development and Growth, and Energy Use*, by John Blodgett and Larry Parker.

[14] On the role of modeling in the first phase, see A Denny Ellerman and Barbara K. Buchner, "The European Union Emissions Trading Scheme: Origins, Allocations, and Early Results," 1 *Environmental Economics and Policy* 1 (Winter 2007), pp. 72-73.

historic data, and data verification. On projecting future emissions, Phase 1 faced uncertainties with respect to economic or sector-based growth rates. Fueled in many cases by over-optimistic economic growth assumptions, these uncertainties increased the probability of inflated business as usual baselines.[15]

The combination of these factors and modest reduction requirements resulted in the emissions allocations for the 2005-2007 trading period being higher than actual 2005 emissions.[16] This result has raised questions about how much reductions achieved during Phase 1 were real as opposed to being merely paper artifacts. On the positive side, verified emissions in 2005 were 3.4% below the estimated 2005 baseline used during the allocation process. In addition, the allowance prices for 2005 stayed persistently high, suggesting some abatement was occurring and raising questions of "windfall" profits. As stated by Ellerman and Buchner:

> First, and most importantly, the persistently high price for EUAs [EU emissions allowance] in a market characterized by sufficient liquidity and sophisticated players must be considered as creating a presumption of abatement. It would be startling if power companies did not incorporate EUA prices into dispatch decisions that would have shifted generation to less emitting plants. There is plenty of anecdotal evidence that this was the case, and the prominent charges of windfall profits assume that the opportunity cost of freely allocated allowances was being passed on (without noting the implications for abatement). Similarly, it would be surprising if there were no changes in production processes that could be made by the operators of industrial plants.[17]

However, EU emissions allowances (EUAs) during Phase 1 did not maintain value. Phase 1 EUAs were basically worthless during the final six months of 2007. This decline in EUA prices at least partially reflected the general non-transferability of Phase 1 EUAs to Phase 2. Only Poland and France included limited banking in their Phase 1 NAPs. The EC further restricted use of Phase 1 EUAs in Phase 2 with a ruling in November, 2006.[18] As a result, excess Phase 1 EUAs were worthless at the end of 2007.[19]

---

[15] Regina Betz and Misato Sato, "Emissions Trading: Lessons Learnt from the 1st Phase of the EU ETS and Prospects for the 2nd Phase," 6 *Climate Policy* (2006), p. 354.

[16] For a further discussion, see *Climate Change: The European Union's Emissions Trading System (EU-ETS)*, CRS Report RL33581, by Larry Parker.

[17] A Denny Ellerman and Barbara K. Buchner, "The European Union Emissions Trading Scheme: Origins, Allocations, and Early Results," 1 *Environmental Economics and Policy* 1 (Winter 2007), p. 83.

[18] European Commission, *Communication from the Commission to the Council and to the European Parliament on the assessment of national allocation plans for the allocation of greenhouse gas emission allowances in the second period of the EU Emissions Trading Scheme,* COM(2006) 725 final, (November 29, 2006), p. 11.

[19] For a further discussion, see Joseph Kruger, Wallace E. Oates, and William A. Pizer, "Decentralization in the EU Emissions Trading Scheme and Lessons for Global Policy, 1 *Environmental Economics and Policy* 1 (Winter 2007), p. 126; and, Frank J. Convery and Luke Redmond, "Market and Price Development in the European Union Emissions Trading
(continued...)

Figure 1. ECX CFI Futures Contracts: Price and Volume

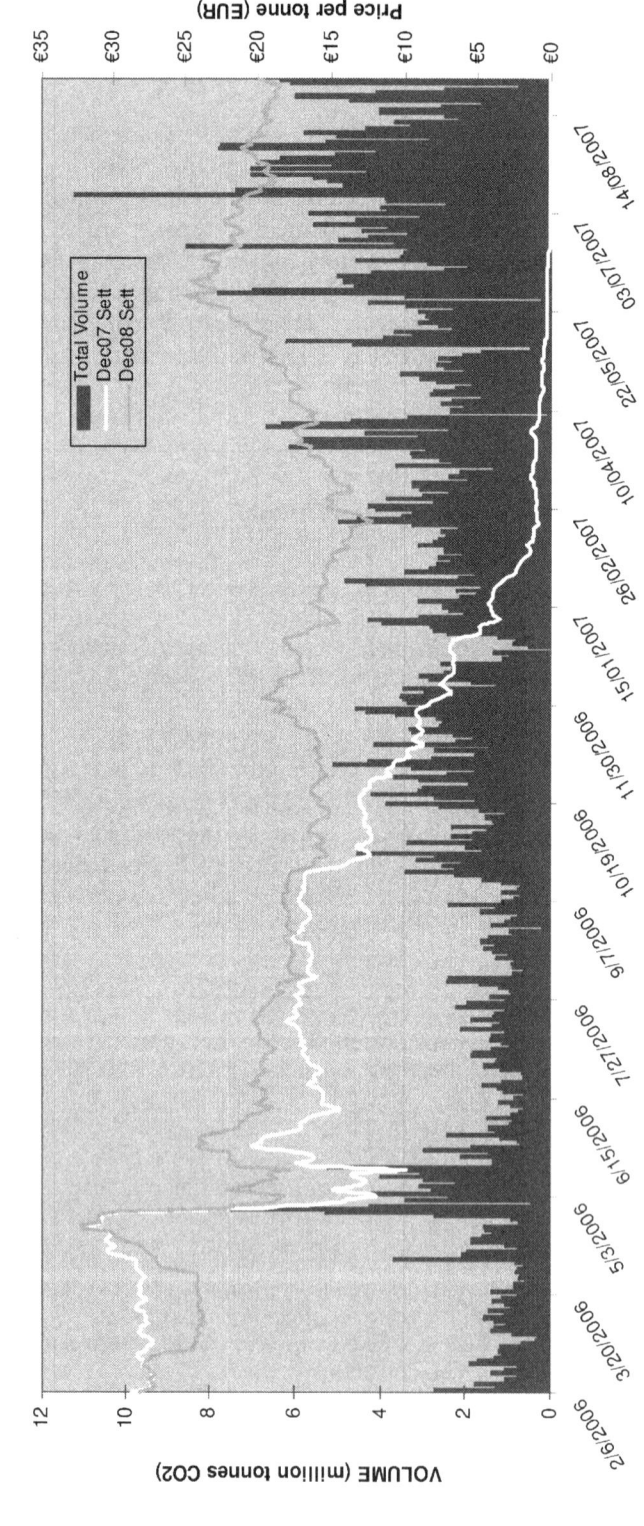

Source: ECX Exchange.

19 (...continued)

Scheme,

One consequence of the non-transferability of Phase 1 EUAs is that prices for Phase 2 EUAs have been firm, as indicated by **Figure 1** above. This firmness may reflect the ability of the EC to certify Phase 2 NAPs using more verifiable baseline data than were available for Phase 1.[20] Scarcity is critical for the proper functioning of an allowance market. A major reason the EC rejected *ex post* adjustments[21] was fear that such adjustments would have a disruptive effect on the marketplace.[22] Phase 1 did not firmly establish this foundation of markets;[23] based on the Phase 2 EUA future's market, further market development appears to be occurring, although several challenges to that development will be discussed later.

Need to Adjust ETS Allocations

While the environmental performance of Phase 1 may be disputed, the need for additional reductions to achieve Kyoto is not. As indicated by the red arrow in **Figure 2**, the EC projects that the EU-15 existing measures will halt the projected increase in greenhouse gases; however, as indicated by the green line, they are insufficient to reduce EU-15 emissions to their Kyoto requirements that begin in 2008. To achieve this target and the additional requirements of the new EU countries, the EU envisions three sources: (1) further reductions by EU-15 countries covered by the EU bubble (the blue arrow), (2) ensuring the new countries remain in compliance with their Kyoto commitments (the purple arrow), and (3) the use of Kyoto mechanisms (Joint Implementation (JI) and Clean Development Mechanism (CDM) and carbon sinks (the green bar).[24] By 2010, EU-27 emissions are projected at 7.5% below Kyoto baseline levels assuming current policies. This reduction is

---

[20] International Emissions Trading Association, "IETA Position Paper on EU ETS Market Functioning," (no date), p. 2.

[21] Once the EC has approved a country's NAP, including the total number of allowances and the allocation to each covered entity, the allocations can not be re-visited. Attempts to include provisions permitting such post-approval adjustments to a facility's allocation have been uniformly rejected by the EC.

[22] European Commission, *Communication from the Commission to the Council and to the European Parliament on the assessment of national allocation plans for the allocation of greenhouse gas emission allowances in the second period of the EU Emissions Trading Scheme,* COM(2006) 725 final, (November 29, 2006), p 8; and, A Denny Ellerman and Barbara K. Buchner, "The European Union Emissions Trading Scheme: Origins, Allocations, and Early Results," 1 *Environmental Economics and Policy* 1 (Winter 2007), p. 71.

[23] On the mixed record of the EU-ETS and the need for allowance scarcity to a functioning emissions market, see Eric Haymann, *EU Emission Trading: Allocation Battles Intensifying,* Deutsche Bank Research (March 6, 2007). For a generally positive view of ETS market development, see Frank J. Convery and Luke Redmond, "Market and Price Development in the European Union Emissions Trading Scheme, 1 *Environmental Economics and Policy* 1 (Winter 2007), pp. 97-106. For a more negative view, see Karsten Neuhoff, Federico Ferrario, Michael Grubb, Etienne Gabel, and Kim Keats, "Emissions Projections 2008-2012 Versus NAPs II," 6 *Climate Policy* 5 (2006), pp. 395-410.

[24] For more information on the Kyoto Protocol mechanisms, see CRS Report RL33826, *Climate Change: The Kyoto Protocol and International Actions,* by Susan Fletcher and Larry Parker.

projected at 11% if additional measures are included. Currently, eighteen countries are projected to meet their requirements without additional control measures.[25] Only three countries are not projected to meet their requirements even with additional planned measures: Denmark, Italy, and Spain.[26]

Figure 2. Actual and Projected Emissions for EU-25 and EU-15

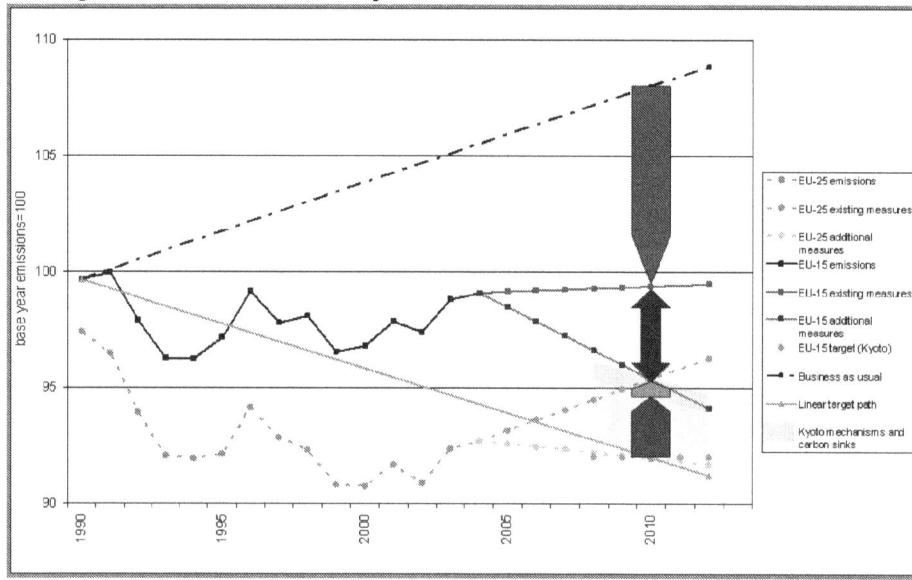

Source: European Commission, *Progress Towards Achieving the Kyoto Objectives*, (October 27, 2006), p. 4.

As indicated by **Table 1** earlier, part of the EC response to the need for additional measures to meet the Kyoto requirements has been to reduce Member States' proposed ETS allocations. In the case of new Members, these reductions have been substantial in some cases. Only four countries — Denmark, France, Slovenia, and the United Kingdom — have had no reductions in their proposed ETS allocations. Other responses include an EC-approved proposal to impose mandatory CO_2 emissions standards on light-duty vehicles.[27]

---

[25] Belgium, Finland, France, Germany, Luxembourg, Netherlands, Sweden, United Kingdom, Bulgaria, Czech Republic, Estonia, Hungary, Latvia, Lithuania, Poland, Romania, Slovak Republic, and Slovenia. Cyprus and Malta are not Annex 1 countries.

[26] European Environmental Agency, *Greenhouse Gas Emission Trends and Projections in Europe 2007* (Copenhagen, 2007), p. 11.

[27] See European Commission, *Proposal for a Regulation of the European Parliament and of the Council: Setting emission performance standards for new passenger cars as part of the Community's integrated approach to reduce CO_2 emissions form light-duty vehicles*, COM(2007) 856 final (December 19, 2007); and, European Commission, *Results of the review of the Community Strategy to reduce CO_2 emissions from passenger cars and light-commercial vehicles*, (Brussels, February 7, 2007).

Issues Arising in NAPs for the ETS

Supplementarity

As noted earlier, for Phase 2, the EC has issued a linking directive permitting the use of Kyoto mechanisms for compliance. Including the linking directive has had beneficial effects on the development of JI and CDM markets and more generally on CO_2 reduction projects in the developing world.[28]

This emerging JI/CDM supply has the potential to largely fill the projected EU-15 shortfall in meeting the Kyoto Protocol requirements.[29] According to the World Bank, the estimated aggregate shortfall ("distance to target") for the EU-15 for Phase 2 ranges from 900-1,500 million metric tonnes of CO_2e (CO_2 equivalent) with an average estimate of 1,250 million. This represents an 8%-10% further reduction from projected levels and is in line with the EU estimated shortfall discussed above.[30] The World Bank cites estimates that 1,000-1,200 million metric tonnes of CO_2e credits from CDM and JI projects are likely to be imported into the EU-ETS: "Put in perspective, it means that installations, using credits from CDM and JI, could be in a balanced position or a marginally short one. In the latter case, fuel switching would help bridge the gap."[31]

However, a potential barrier to this scenario is the "supplementarity" requirements of the Kyoto Protocol which is embodied in criterion 12 of the EC NAP approval process. Supplementarity requires that developed countries, such as most EU countries, ensure that their use of JI/CDM credits is supplemental to their own domestic control efforts. In defining supplementarity for Phase 2, the EC has used 10% of a country's allowance allocation as a rule of thumb in approving NAPs — with a greater limit possible based on a country's domestic efforts to reduce emissions. As indicated in **Table 2**, this process has resulted in some significant reductions in some countries' proposed limits (e.g., Ireland, Poland, Spain), but some increase in others (e.g., Italy, Latvia, Lithuania). Although these reductions appear substantial in individual cases, most analysts agree that they do not represent a major barrier to the cost-effective use of JI/CDM. As stated by the World Bank:

> The Commission assessed NAPs for imports of carbon assets (including planned and substantiated governmental purchases) ostensibly with a view to limit

---

[28] A Denny Ellerman and Barbara K. Buchner, "The European Union Emissions Trading Scheme: Origins, Allocations, and Early Results," 1 *Environmental Economics and Policy* 1 (Winter 2007), p. 84. Also, see International Emissions Trading Association, "IETA Position Paper on EU ETS Market Functioning," (no date), p. 2.

[29] The ten other Annex 1 EU countries (mostly Eastern European "economies in transition") are estimated by the World Bank to have an excess of Assigned Amount Units (AAUs) of 700-1,500 million metric tonnes of CO2e. The two other EU countries — Cyprus and Malta — are non-Annex 1 countries.

[30] The World Bank, *State and Trends of the Carbon Market 2007*, (Washington, D.C., May 2007) pp. 14-16, 39-40.

[31] Ibid., p. 16.

imports to no more than 50% of the "expected distance to target" for each Member State. According to the vast majority of analysts, this does not place any practical constraints on the demand for CDM/JI from EU installations: The market received the November 2006 EU decision to impose tighter caps with an immediate increase in the price of EUA-II, while uncertainty at that time about supplementarity caps immediately dampened prices for CERs [i.e., CDM credits] (secondary CER market reacted more quickly than the more stable primary market).[32]

Table 2. JI/CDM Limits for Phase 2: 2008-2012

Member State	Proposed JI/CDM Limit (% of allocation)	Approved JI/CDM Limit (% of allocation)
Austria	20%	10%
Belgium	8%	8.4%
Bulgaria	20%	12.6%
Czech Rep.	10%	10%
Cyprus	(not included)	10%
Denmark	19%	17%
Estonia	0	0
Finland	12%	10%
France	10%	13.5%
Germany	12%	20%
Greece	9%	9%
Hungary	10%	10%
Ireland	50%	10%
Italy	25%	15%
Latvia	5%	10%
Lithuania	9%	20%
Luxembourg	10%	10%
Malta	(not included)	(to be determined)
Netherlands	12%	10%
Poland	25%	10%

---

[32] Ibid., p. 16.

Member State	Proposed JI/CDM Limit (% of allocation)	Approved JI/CDM Limit (% of allocation)
Portugal	10% (50% in some cases)	10%
Romania	10%	10%
Slovakia	7%	7%
Slovenia	(not included)	15.8%
Spain	39%	20%
Sweden	20%	10%
United Kingdom	8%	8%

Source: Source: European Commission, "Emissions Trading: EU-wide cap for 2008-2012 set at 2.08 billion allowances after assessment of national plans for Bulgaria," EC Press Release, October 26, 2007. Proposed JI/CDM Limits from Cambridge University, *Second Phase National Allocation Plans: A Comparative Analysis*, at [http://www.econ.cam.ac.uk/research/tsec/euets/].

The advantage of EU access to the JI/CDM market is lower costs under current market conditions. In 2006, guaranteed CDM and JI credits sold at a 10%-30% discount to EUAs, a discount that reflects risks involved in CDM/JI transactions. The degree to which this discount continues depends to some degree on the efforts of participating governments and the CDM and JI Executive Boards to streamline procedures and regulations, firm up methodological assessments, and integrate the different markets. The Chinese government has set a credit price floor of 8-9 euro — price setting that reflects its dominant role in the CDM market.[33] The ability of CDM host countries to raise this floor to reflect more fully the 18-20 euro EUA price depends on supply. In contrast to the World Bank, Point Carbon reports that its survey of respondents claimed that CDM/JI supply will be insufficient to meet EU demand. As a result, price will be set by the marginal cost of EU domestic emissions reductions (which in turn sets the ceiling on EUA prices). The availability of JI/CDM credits will reduce that marginal cost (reducing the price of EUAs), but the survey suggests that JI/CDM prices are likely to rise.[34] In contrast, if the JI/CDM availability exceeds the need of the EU, the price would be set by the marginal cost of JI/CDM credit supply — a considerably lower price as reflected by the Chinese price floor.

Some observers praise the broadening and increased flexibility that CDM and JI represent in helping Annex 1 countries meet their Kyoto requirements. The World Bank argues that the flexibility enshrined in the Kyoto flexibility mechanisms and other market mechanisms (e.g., banking) is a superior "safety valve" for cost concerns than a price cap as suggested in some U.S. legislation. As stated by the World Bank:

---

[33] In 2006, China supplied 70% of CDM credits. Point Carbon, *Carbon 2007*, (March 13, 2007), p. 18.

[34] Ibid., p. 42.

Flexibility is key to ensuring that there is a built-in safety valve for compliance without resort to market distortion through price caps.... It would be appropriate to recall here that flexibility is not the goal of climate policy; rather it is a tool to help achieve the most stringent targets. In this regard, the use of flexibility mechanisms in Phase II coupled with much stronger reductions in Phase III and the unilateral European target announced for 2020 should be at stringent enough levels that can help stimulate a low carbon clean investment future. Setting an arbitrary price cap distorts the level of innovation required to meet the compliance target and dilutes the ability to meet the environment target [footnote omitted].[35]

In contrast, some environmental groups are concerned that widespread use of CDM and JI will prevent the investment in domestic efforts that the Kyoto Protocol envisioned and that will be necessary as emission caps become more stringent and more countries participate.[36] In addition to concerns about the volume of outside credits that may be used in the ETS, there are issues over the quality of the credits, particularly with respect to "additionality" — the requirement in the Kyoto Protocol that project credits represent reductions that would not have occurred in the absence of the CDM program. In expressing concern about CDM not being additional to current policies, WWF-UK states: "It is important to remember that CDM projects do not themselves reduce net global greenhouse gas emissions — they merely allow the project investor to pollute more at home. Ensuring that projects are additional is therefore crucial to maintaining the environmental integrity of the whole system as a breach of this means that global emissions actually increase."[37] Such concerns may prevent full exploitation of CDM opportunities for some time.

Auction Policy

In general, allowances have been allocated free to participating entities under the ETS. During Phase 1, The EU-ETS Directive allowed countries to auction up to 5% of allowance allocations, rising to 10% under Phase 2.[38] Under Phase 1, only four of twenty-five countries used auctions at all, and only Denmark auctioned the full 5%. The political difficulty in instituting significant auctioning into ETS allowance allocations is the almost universal agreement by covered entities in favor of free allocation of allowances and opposition to auctions.[39] Free allocation of allowances represents a one-time transfer of wealth to the entities receiving them

---

[35] The World Bank, *State and Trends of the Carbon Market 2007* (Washington, DC, May 2007), p. 39.

[36] For example, see World Wildlife Fund — UK, *Emission Impossible: Access to JI/CDM Credits in phase II of the EU Emissions Trading Scheme* (June, 2007).

[37] Ibid., p. 7.

[38] For a further discussion of auctioning and the ETS, see Cameron Hepburn, *et. al.*, "Auctioning of EU ETS phase II allowances: how and why?" 6 *Climate Policy* (2006), pp. 137-160.

[39] A Denny Ellerman and Barbara K. Buchner, "The European Union Emissions Trading Scheme: Origins, Allocations, and Early Results," 1 *Environmental Economics and Policy* 1 (Winter 2007), p. 73.

from the government issuing them.[40] The resulting transfer of wealth has been described by several analysts as "windfall profits."[41] As summarized by Ellerman and Buchner: "Allocation in the EU ETS provides one more example that, notwithstanding the advice of economists, the free allocation of allowances is not to be easily set aside."[42]

Despite concerns about windfall profits and economic distortions resulting from the free allocation of allowances, there is little change in basic allocation philosophy for Phase 2. No country proposed auctioning the maximum percentage of allowances allowed (10%). Most do not include auctions at all.[43] The unwillingness of governments to employ auctions as an allocating mechanism revolve around equity considerations, including: (1) inability of some covered entities to pass through cost because of regulation or exposure to international competition; (2) potential drag on a sector's economic performance from the up-front cost of auctioned allowances; and, (3) the potential that government will not recycle revenues to alleviate compliance costs, international competitiveness impacts, or other equity concerns, resulting in the auction costs being the same as a tax.[44]

Against these concerns, economic analysis provides several arguments in favor of auctions in general, and in the case of the EU ETS in particular. General arguments in favor of auctions include:[45]

- Purest embodiment of the "polluter pays" principle;

- Reduces distributional distortions that free allocation (and accompanying "windfall profits") can create;

- Creates a "level playing field" for existing and new covered entities;

---

[40] Joseph Kruger, Wallace E. Oates, and William A. Pizer, "Decentralization in the EU Emissions Trading Scheme and Lessons for Global Policy," 1 *Environmental Economics and Policy* 1 (Winter 2007), p. 114.

[41] E.g., Deutsche Bank Research, *EU Emission Trading: Allocation Battles Intensifying*, (March 6, 2007) pp. 2-3; and, Regina Betz and Misato Sato, "Emissions Trading: Lessons Learnt from the 1st Phase of the EU ETS and Prospects for the 2nd Phase", 6 *Climate Policy* (2006), p. 353.

[42] A Denny Ellerman and Barbara K. Buchner, "The European Union Emissions Trading Scheme: Origins, Allocations, and Early Results," 1 *Environmental Economics and Policy* 1 (Winter 2007), p. 85.

[43] For a review of proposed NAP 2 auction proposals as of January 12, 2007, see Karsten Neuhoff, *EU ETS Auction Workshop*, (Cambridge, January 12th, 2007), p. 26.

[44] Martina Priebe, *Distributional Effect of Carbon-allowance Trading*, (Cambridge, January 12, 2007). Also, see Eurochambres, *Review of the EU Emission Trading System* (June, 2007), p. 5.

[45] Michael Grubb, *The Growing Role of Auctioning in the Economy? Or Allocation Theory and the Practice in Europe: the Great Divide*, (Paris, September 25, 2006), p 4.

- Gives the potential for reducing the impact of compliance on the economy as a whole if auction revenues are used to reduce more distorting taxes on investment (i.e., "double dividend"); and

- Can improve emission market liquidity and transparency.

In the case of the EU-ETS, the use of free allocations rather than auctions has created some perverse incentives for covered entities and unnecessary complexity to the ETS. As discussed later in more detail, providing allowances free to existing entities can encourage the continued use of inefficient plant, and reduce the incentive for investing in efficiency improvements. The degree to which this occurs depends on the specific allocation approach taken. In contrast, an auction can help create a price floor, particularly if coupled with a reserve price, that encourages development of new technologies and efficiency improvements in existing plant.

A free allocation scheme generally has to make some provision for new entrants in addition to allocating allowances to existing entities. It also raises issues with respect to existing sources that later decide to shutdown. This added complexity to the ETS is discussed next.

New Entrant Reserves

Unlike previous cap and trade programs, the Member States of the EU have included provisions for the allocation of allowances to new entrants to the system.[46] The reasoning behind this decision is based on equity: (1) it isn't fair to allocate allowances free to existing entities while requiring new entrants to purchase them, and (2) the EU doesn't want to put Member States at a disadvantage in competing for new investments.[47] These equity concerns trumped concerns about economic efficiency.

As is the case for existing entities, the free allocation of allowances to new entrants is a subsidy. For the ETS, the size and distribution of this subsidy is left to the individual Member States. For Phase 1, the reserve varied widely from the average of 3% of total allowances: Poland set aside only 0.4% of its allocation for new entrants while Malta set aside 26%. For Phase 2, the spread continues with Poland reserving 3.2% of its allowances for new entrant in contrast to 45% proposed by Latvia.[48]

---

[46] For example, the U.S. acid rain program provides no allocation of allowances to new entrants; instead, an EPA sanctioned auction is held annually to ensure that allowances are available to new entrants. New entrants can also obtain allowances from existing sources willing to sell them, either directly, through the EPA auction, or via a broker.

[47] A Denny Ellerman and Barbara K. Buchner, "The European Union Emissions Trading Scheme: Origins, Allocations, and Early Results," 1 *Environmental Economics and Policy* 1 (Winter 2007), p. 75.

[48] Karoline Rogge, Joachim Schleich, and Regina Betz, *An Early Assessment of National Allocation Plans for Phase 2 of EU Emission Trading*, Fraunhofer Institute System and Innovation Research (January 2006).

The decision to employ a new entrant reserve adds complexity to Member States' allocation plans and influences the investment decisions of covered entities. Rules have to be promulgated with respect to the reserve's size, manner in which the allowances are dispensed, and how to proceed if the demand either exceeds the supply, or vice versa. As indicated, countries have not harmonized new entrant reserve rules with respect to size. Likewise, there is no standardization on dispensing allowances and replenishing the reserve: first-come, first-serve with no replenishment is one approach used, but a variety of procedures have been developed both to dispense allowances and to replenish the reserve if supply is inadequate.[49] Member States also have different formulas for determining how many allowances a new entrant should receive. Member States claim to use a form of "benchmarking" to determine allowance allocations — an approach based on a standard of "best practices" or "best technology" that is applied to the new entrant's anticipated production or capacity. However, the definitions and application of the benchmarks used by the Member States are not uniform.

This diversity in approaches to addressing new entrants results in technology or fuel-specific subsidies, which vary by country. **Table 3** presents the results of a study of the value of annual allocations for a natural gas combined-cycle power plant under different countries' Phase 2 new entrant allocation rules. Assuming an allowance value of 10 euro, the plant's allocation would vary between 0 in Sweden (no free allocation) to 11 million euro annually in Germany.[50] At the current Phase 2 allowance price of 20 euro, this annual subsidy is equivalent to the fixed annual costs of the power plant.[51] Subsidies of this magnitude are likely to affect investment decisions. As noted by Schleich, Betz, and Rogge, these subsidies: "run counter to the logic of emission trading systems, where market prices and flexibility are supposed to guide investment decisions rather than subsidies for particular types of installations."[52]

---

[49] For a summary of 18 proposed NAPs with respect to new entrant reserves, see ibid., pp. 46-47.

[50] Markus Ahman and Kristina Holmgren, "New entrant allocation in the Nordic energy sectors: incentives and options in the EU ETS," 6 *Climate Policy* (2006), p. 430.

[51] Ibid., p. 431. Estimated at 19.5 million euro (2003$).

[52] Joachim Schleich, Regina Betz, and Karoline Rogge, *EU Emissions Trading — Better Job Second Time Around?* Fraunhofer Institute System and Innovation Research (February, 2007), p. 23.

Table 3. Value of Annual Allocation for New NGCC Powerplant
(millions of euro, allowance price of 10 euro)

Country	Value of Free Allocation
Finland	2.7
Germany	11.0
Latvia	8.3
Lithuania	10.0
Poland	10.3
Sweden	0.0

Source: Markus Ahman and Kristina Holmgren, "New entrant allocation in the Nordic energy sectors: incentives and options in the EU ETS," 6 *Climate Policy* (2006), p. 430.

Closure Policy

The reverse side of the new entrant allocation issue is the what to do with the allocations to existing plants that shut down. Under U.S. cap and trade programs, those allowances are retained by the company, based on the assumption that a new power plant will be built to replace the closed one. For most countries in the ETS, closure policy is directly linked to the new entrant reserve: allowances allocated to existing sources that shut down are fed into the entrant reserve to be allocated to new sources. Thus, free allowances to existing facilities are tied to continued operation of that facility. One reason for this approach may be the multiple country aspect of the ETS and the political fear that owners of facilities could shut down plants in one country, keep the allowance allocation, and move to another Member State.[53]

Unfortunately, this closure policy encourages inefficient facilities to continue operating to maintain the subsidy the free allowance allocation represents. As examined by Ahman, et al.:

> The withdrawal of allocation based on reduced economic activity or closure makes the loss of the allocation into an additional opportunity cost affecting the production decision. In considering the marginal cost of operation, the firm will recognize that it receives the allocation *if and only if* it continues to operate. Consequently, the firm will not maximize its profits only with respect to the cost of production (including resource cost and the opportunity cost of allowances); in addition, it will take into account the value of the allowances that it will lose should it cease to produce output. Imposing a condition that the allocation

[53] Ibid., p. 19.

depends on continued operation of the installation transform the allocation into a production subsidy [footnote omitted].[54]

One response to the perverse incentives of the closure rule has been pioneered by Germany and adopted by a few countries. Under the "transfer rule," owners of existing facilities being shut down can transfer the allocation from that facility to a new replacement facility.[55] For Phase 1, seven countries — Germany, Greece, Hungary, Luxembourg, the Netherlands, Poland, and the UK — included transfer rules in their NAP. For Phase 2, Cyprus, Flanders (part of Belgium), and Malta have joined in including such rules in their NAPs.[56]

Benchmarking

A third aspect of free allocation is benchmarking. As noted earlier, for new entrants benchmarking involves allocating allowances based on a standard of "best practices" or "best technology" that is applied to the new entrant's anticipated production or capacity. Environmental and other groups have advocated the expansion of benchmarking to allocations for existing facilities in addition to new entrants. However, benchmarking is very difficult given the diversity of processes involved and subject to manipulation in favor of one technology or fuel-source over another. For example, The Netherlands made a serous attempt to use benchmarks in its allocation scheme, but abandoned the effort after 125 benchmarks were developed.[57]

Benchmarks can also be used to encourage investment in one fuel-source over another. This issue has arisen in the case of Germany's proposed Phase 2 NAP. As part of Germany's overall energy policy, the NAP provides for the "fuel-neutral" allocation of allowances to new powerplants based on benchmarks reflecting current best practice for each fuel. For a coal-fired facility, the benchmark is 750 grams CO_2/Kwh reflecting a conversion efficiency of 45%. For natural gas-fired facility, the benchmark is 365 grams CO_2/Kwh, reflecting a conversion efficiency of 55%. These are benchmarks that current technology can achieve without the addition of any carbon capture and sequestration technology or purchase of offsets from other sources. In addition, the government proposed to provide new entrants with a guaranteed allocation of allowances based on actual emissions for 10 years after a 4 year allocation based on an 85% capacity factor. As a result, the NAP would provide almost no incentive to utilities to reduce CO_2 emissions by fuel shifting, and to

[54] Markus Ahman, Dallas Burtraw, Joseph Kruger, Lars Zetterberg, "A Ten-Year Rule to guide the allocation of EU emission allowances," 35 *Energy Policy* (2007), p. 1721.

[55] For a further discussion of the German NAP II, see Christoph Kuhleis, *The German NAP II* (London, September 13, 2006).

[56] Joachim Schleich, Regina Betz, and Karoline Rogge, *EU Emissions Trading — Better Job Second Time Around?* Fraunhofer Institute System and Innovation Research (February, 2007), p. 19.

[57] A Denny Ellerman and Barbara K. Buchner, "The European Union Emissions Trading Scheme: Origins, Allocations, and Early Results," 1 *Environmental Economics and Policy* 1 (Winter 2007), p. 77.

essentially encourage the use of lignite — Germany's most abundant and least expensive fossil fuel.[58] This policy reflects concerns about Germany becoming too dependent on imported Russian natural gas, the price of which tracks oil.[59] Indeed, economic analysis suggests that the price of an EUA would have to reach 45 euro before lower-carbon emitting natural gas-fired facilities become more economic than coal.[60] As summarized by German utility RWE's chief financial officer:

> The name of our oil is lignite. We want to develop this energy source using new technology and based on environmentally friendly processes. However, governments will have to create the right political framework for this to occur.[61]

In reviewing the German proposed NAP, the EC disapproved the guarantee of allowances to new entrants that extended beyond the Kyoto compliance period (2008-2012), but approved the fuel-specific allocation formulas.[62]

Allocation and Energy Policy

As suggested above, the conflict between national energy policies and the free workings of a carbon market are reflected in most countries' allocation schemes. The combination of free allocations to existing facilities and new entrants, along with closure and benchmarking policies, allow countries to maintain substantial control over energy policy and related economic investment regardless of the price signals the carbon market might send if the market economics of carbon emission reductions were the sole determinant of future investments. This control has been used to preserve existing investment and jobs, encourage exploitation of domestic resources (e.g., coal, lignite) and lower energy prices. Economists argue that such a strategy

---

[58] Klaus Traube, *Germany's NAP — Perspectives of Concerned Actors*, (Salzburg, September 30, 2004), p. 5. As noted by the EC: this approach "encourages investment in new power plants but not automatically in low CO2 emitting ones." European Commission, *Questions and Answers on Emissions Trading and National Allocation Plants for 2008 to 2012* (Brussels, November 29, 2006) p. 4.

[59] Reported by Vera Eckert, "Germany's Coal Power Plans Threaten EU Climate Goal," Reuter News Service, (May 15, 2007).

[60] Analysis by Booz Allen as reported by Vera Eckert, "Germany's Coal Power Plans Threaten EU Climate Goal," Reuter News Service, (May 15, 2007).

[61] Statement of Klaus Sturany, "RWE Slams German NAP Decision," *Carbon Finance*, (March 16, 2007), p. 1.

[62] European Commission, *On the assessment of National Allocation Plans for the allocation of greenhouse gas emission allowances in the second period of the EU Emission Trading Scheme accompanying Commission Decision of 29 November 2006 on the National Allocation Plans of Germany, Greece, Ireland, Latvia, Lithuania, Luxembourg, Malta, Slovakia, Sweden and the United Kingdom in accordance with Directive 2003/87/EC.* (Brussels, November 29, 2006).

is based on an economic misconception about how prices are set,[63] and is inherently contradictory. As stated by Deutsche Bank Research:

> The political objective frequently expressed in both the EU and Germany of achieving lower energy prices at the same time as implementing climate protection measures should be rejected. The objectives of climate protection and lower energy prices (for fossil fuels) are contradictory. Higher energy prices are desirable from an ecological point of view. Although more competition in the electricity and gas sectors could — ceteris paribus — lead to a reduction in prices, this will probably be more than outweighed in the medium term by rising commodity prices and higher fiscal burdens. In this respect, more honesty is needed from all parties.[64]

The EC has put some limitations on country's efforts to influence investment, including disallowing any *ex post* adjustments and allowance guarantees. As noted above, the EC explicitly disallows any provision of a country's NAP that guarantees allowances to covered entities beyond the phase for which the allowances are allocated. The EC argues that allocation guarantees give such installations an unfair advantage over other installations that do not get such guarantees.[65]

Proponents of allocation guarantees argue it is difficult to plan new investment based on five-year allowance allocations.[66] Yet, it is precisely the long term effects of new investments and the potential that they will lock-in high carbon emitting technologies that worry some, including the EC and member governments. As stated in the *Stern Review*:

> The next 10 to 20 years will be a period of transition, from a world where carbon-pricing schemes are in their infancy, to one where carbon pricing is universal and is automatically factored into decision making. In this transitional period, while the credibility of policy is still being established and the international framework is taking shape, it is critical that governments consider how to avoid the risks of locking into a high-carbon infrastructure, including

---

[63] As stated by Cameron Hepburn, et al., in the context of auctions: "One of the widest economic misconceptions about auctioning is that it would simply add costs which would be passed through to 'downstream' companies and consumers. [footnoted example omitted]. Yet, if firms maximize profits, then even with free allocation they pass on the opportunity costs of allowances to downstream prices. Changing from free allocation to auctioning will have little impact on product prices. [further explanatory footnote omitted] However, because auctioning raises revenue that may be reallocated, it has, *prima facie*, the *potential* to correct distributional impacts." Cameron Hepburn, et al., "Auctioning of EU ETS phase II allowances: how and why?" 6 *Climate Policy* (2006), p. 140.

[64] Deutsche Bank Research, *EU Emission Trading: Allocation Battles Intensifying* (March 6, 2007) p. 8.

[65] European Commission, *Questions and Answers on Emissions Trading and National Allocation Plans for 2008 to 2012* (Brussels, November 29, 2006), pp. 3-4.

[66] For example, see "RWE slams German NAP decision," Reported in Carbon Finance (March 16, 2007).

considering whether any additional measures may be justified to reduce the risks.[67]

Avoiding locking-in high carbon energy technology by encouraging deployment of advanced low carbon energy technology under the ETS would involve two elements: (1) reducing behavioral distortion resulting from the current free allocation system, and (2) energy pricing that reflects carbon costs. As indicated by the previous discussions, the NAP 2 submitted to and approved by the EC generally have not reduced the distortions from the free allowance system. The primary means of reducing such distortions would be to increase the use of auctions and/or by more extensive use of benchmarking based on capacity alone (not differentiated by fuel source). As indicated above, no country has submitted a NAP that requires the full 10% auctioning allowed by the EC for Phase 2, although the number of countries auctioning at least some percentage of their allocations has grown from four in Phase 1 to nine in Phase 2. In addition, the EC allows countries to institute or expand auctions at any time without its pre-approval. Uniform benchmarks are also rare with only four countries intending to use them to any significant degree.[68]

With respect to a price signal for energy development, the Phase 1 experience was instructive with respect to the value of accurate emissions inventories and registries, but not in terms of developing a price floor that would stimulate development of new technology. One mechanism to develop such a floor, banking, was not used extensively during Phase 1; indeed, as noted earlier, the lack of Phase 1 to Phase 2 banking contributed to the collapse in Phase 1 prices in 2007. It is likely to be far more important in Phase 2.

In the context of the ETS, options to provide a price floor beyond banking include expanding use of auctions (including incorporating a reserve price into auctions), financial instruments (such as options and futures contracts), and expansion of industries covered by the ETS. The EC is moving very slowly with respect to auctions, despite support for them by environmental groups and economists. Financial instruments are being made available to entities by the major

---

[67] Nicholas Stern, *The Economics of Climate Change: The Stern Review* (Cambridge, 2006), p. xix. As stated by the EC with respect to fossil fuel power plants: "The expectations of higher costs associated with CCS-equipped power plants after 2020 give rise to a tangible risk. This is the risk of a "non-CCS technology lock-in" as the result of ill-considered investment decisions with respect to the coal-fired capacity due for replacement in the coming 10-15 years. It is imperative to avoid a situation where much of the new build before 2020 is undertaken in a way that would either preclude or insufficiently guarantee the addition of CCS components on a sufficiently wide scale after 2020." European Commission, *Sustainable power generation from fossil fuels: aiming for near-zero emissions from coal after 2020* (Brussels, January 10, 2007), p. 7.

[68] Joachim Schleich, Regina Betz, and Karoline Rogge, *EU Emissions Trading — Better Job Second Time Around?* Fraunhofer Institute System and Innovation Research (February, 2007), p. 17.

emission exchange, although not extensively used as of yet.[69] It is the third option, expanding coverage, that the EU has stated as an important goal for Phase 3.[70]

With respect to longer-term planning and investment, the EC apparently agrees that a five-year allowance allocation may be too short and believes that in order to provide greater predictability for long-term investment decisions, a longer allocation period should be considered for Phase 3.[71]

Expansion

Despite the EC interest in expanding the ETS, its coverage in terms of industries included for Phase 2 is essentially the same as for Phase 1. The potential exception is for aviation. In December, 2006, the EC proposed bringing greenhouse gas emissions from civil aviation into the ETS in two phases.[72] In 2011, the proposal would cover flights within the EU; in 2012, the coverage would expand to include all flights to and from EU airports. EU and foreign airplane operators would be included. This proposal is subject to approval by the European Parliament and The Council of the European Union.

In discussing future climate change activities, the EC has identified two other areas for possible inclusion under the ETS: (1) methane emissions from gas engines, and from coal, oil and gas production; and (2) nitrous oxide emissions from large combustion facilities.[73] However, their incorporation into the ETS will not occur before 2013 at the earliest.

Harmonization

The improved emissions inventories resulting from Phase 1 have allowed the EC to harmonize the types of installations covered by the ETS across the various Member States.[74] In addition, as noted above, the EC has imposed a uniform rule on the Member States preventing the use of *ex-post* adjustments. However, the above discussion also suggests that the ETS enters Phase 2 having made little advancement

---

[69] For example, see European Climate Exchange, *The Carbon Market: How to Trade ECX Emissions Contracts* (July 2007).

[70] European Commission, *Limiting Global Change to 2 degrees Celsius: The Way Ahead for 2020 and Beyond*, (Brussels, January 10, 2007), pp. 6-7.

[71] Ibid., p. 6.

[72] European Commission, *Proposal for a Directive of the European Parliament and of the Council amending Directive 2003/87/EC so as to include aviation activities in the scheme for greenhouse gas emission allowance trading within the Community*, (Brussels, December 12, 2006).

[73] European Commission, *Limiting Global Change to 2 Degrees Celsius: The Way Ahead for 2020 and Beyond* (Brussels, January 10, 2007), p. 7.

[74] Ibid., p. 23.

in harmonizing individual countries' allocations schemes.[75] As with Phase 1, countries will continue to differ widely on the use of auctions; design and use of benchmarks; design, size, and allocation for new entrant reserves; and rules for closure during Phase 2.

The expansion of the EU to 27 Member States and the EC's desire to enlarge the ETS promise to test the willingness of the EC, Member governments, industry, and environmental groups to harmonize and improve the efficiency of allocation rules. Currently, there is no consensus on the specifics of any harmonized rules. The EC has stated that one of its goals is by 2020 to "harmonise allocation processes across Member States to achieve undistorted competition across Europe, including through a wider use of auctioning."[76] Experience with Phase 1 and Phase 2 NAPs suggests this may be a slow process.

Summary and Considerations for U.S. Cap-and-Trade Proposals

The United States is not a party to the Kyoto Protocol and no legislative proposal before the Congress would impose as stringent an emission reduction regime on the United States as Kyoto would have. However, through almost three years of carbon emissions trading the EU has gained valuable experience as it prepares for Kyoto. This experience, along with the process of developing Phase 2 NAPs, may provide some insight into current cap-and-trade design issues in the U.S.

Emission Inventories and Target Setting

The ETS experience with market trading and target setting confirms once again the central importance of a credible emissions inventory to a functioning cap-and-trade program.[77] The lack of credible EU-wide data on emissions was a direct cause of the ETS Phase 1 allowance market collapse in 2006. Arguably, the most important result of Phase 1 was the development of a credible inventory on which to base future targets and NAPs.

In the United States, section 821 of the 1990 Clean Air Act Amendments requires electric generating facilities affected by the acid rain provisions of Title IV

---

[75] Joachim Schleich, Regina Betz, and Karoline Rogge, *EU Emissions Trading — Better Job Second Time Around?* Fraunhofer Institute System and Innovation Research (February 2007), p. 23.

[76] European Commission, *Limiting Global Change to 2 degrees Celsius: The way ahead for 2020 and beyond*, (Brussels, January 10, 2007), p. 6.

[77] As stated by CRS in 1992: "For an economic incentive system to be effective, several preconditions are necessary. Perhaps the most important is data about the emissions being controlled. Such data are important to levy any tax, allocate any permits, and enforce any limit." CRS Issue Brief IB92125, *Global Climate: Proposed Economic Mechanisms for Reducing CO_2*, by Larry Parker (archived November 16, 1994), p. 9.

to monitor carbon dioxide in accordance with EPA regulations.[78] This provision was enacted for the stated purpose of establishing a national carbon dioxide monitoring system.[79] As promulgated by EPA, regulations permit owners and operators of affected facilities to monitor their carbon dioxide emissions through either continuous emission monitoring (CEM) or fuel analysis.[80] The CEM regulations for carbon dioxide are similar to those for the acid rain program's sulfur dioxide CEM regulations. Those choosing fuel analysis must calculate mass emissions on a daily, quarterly, and annual basis, based on amounts and types of fuel used. As suggested by the EU-ETS experience, expanding equivalent data requirements to all facilities covered under a cap-and-trade program would be the foundation for developing the allocation systems, reduction targets, and enforcement provisions.

Coverage

Despite economic analysis to the contrary, the EU decided to restrict ETS coverage to six sectors that represent about 45% of the EU's CO_2 emissions.[81] This restriction was estimated to raise the cost of complying with Kyoto from 6 billion euro annually to 6.9 billion euro (1999 euro) compared with a comprehensive trading program. A variety of practical, political, and scientific reasons were given by the EC for the decision.[82]

The experience of the ETS up to now suggests that adding new sectors to an existing trading program is a difficult process. As noted above, a stated goal of the EC is to expand the coverage of the ETS. However, the experience of Phase 1 did not result in the addition of any new sectors going into Phase 2. The only possibility of expanded coverage during Phase 2 is the proposed addition of aviation.

U.S. cap-and-trade proposals generally fall into one of two categories.[83] Most bills are more comprehensive than the ETS, covering 80% to 100% of the country's greenhouse gas emissions. At a minimum, they include the electric utility, transportation, and industrial sectors; disagreement among the bills center on the agricultural sector and smaller commercial and residential sources. In some cases discretion is provided EPA to exempt sources if serious data, economic, or other considerations dictate such a resolution.

---

[78] Section 821, *1990 Clean Air Act Amendments* (P.L. 101-549, 42 USC 7651k).

[79] S.Rept. 101-952.

[80] See 40 CFR 75.13, along with appendix G (for CEMs specifications) and appendix F (for fuel analysis specifications.

[81] For more background, see CRS Report RL33581, *Climate Change: The European Union's Emissions Trading System (EU-ETS),* by Larry Parker.

[82] Ibid., p 3.

[83] For an overview of cap-and-trade proposals, see CRS Report RL33846, *Greenhouse Gas Reduction: Cap-and-Trade Bills in the 110th Congress*, by Larry Parker and Brent D. Yacobucci. For an overview of multi-pollutant control bills, see CRS Report RL34018, *Air Quality: Multi-pollutant Legislation in the 110th Congress*, by Larry Parker and John E. Blodgett.

A second category of bills focuses on the electric utility industry, representing about 33% of U.S. greenhouse gases and therefore less comprehensive than the ETS. Sometimes including additional controls on non-greenhouse gas pollutants, these bills focus on the sources with the most experience with emission trading and the best emissions data. Other sources could be added as circumstances dictate.

As noted, the EU's experience with the ETS suggests that adding sectors to an emission trading scheme can be a slow and contentious process. If one believes that the electric utility sector is a cost-effective place to start addressing greenhouse gas emissions and that there is sufficient time to do the necessary groundwork to eventually add other sectors, then a phased-in approach may be reasonable. If one believes that the economy as a whole needs to begin adjusting to a carbon-constrained environment to meet long term goals, then a more comprehensive approach may be justified. The ETS experience suggests the process doesn't necessarily get any easier if you wait.

Allocation Schemes

Setting up a tradeable allowance system is a lot like setting up a new currency.[84] Allocating allowances is essentially allocating money with the marketplace determining the exchange rate. As noted above, analysis of the free allocation scheme used in the ETS has resulted in "windfall profits" being received by allowance recipients. As stated quite forcefully by Deutsche Bank Research:

> The most striking market outcome of emissions trading to date has been the power industry's windfall profits, which have sparked controversy. We are all familiar with the background: emissions allowances were handed out free of charge to those plant operators participating in the emissions trading scheme. Nevertheless, in particular the producers of electricity succeeded in marking up the market price of electricity to include the opportunity-cost value of the allowances. This is correct from an accounting point of view, since the allowances do have a value and could otherwise be sold. Moreover, emissions trading cannot work without price signals.[85]

The free allocation of allowances in the ETS incorporates two other mechanisms that create perverse incentives and significant distortions in the emissions markets: new entrant reserves and closure policy. Combined with an uncoordinated and spotty benchmarking approach for both new and existing sources, the result is a greenhouse gas reduction scheme that is influenced more by national policy than by the emissions marketplace.

The most discussed alternative allocation scheme in the ETS is the expanded use of auctions: this approach could simplify allocation and permit market forces to influence compliance strategies more fully. Most countries did not employ auctions

---

[84] Unlike a carbon tax which uses the existing currency system to control emissions — be it euro or dollars.

[85] Deutsche Bank Research, *EU Emission Trading: Allocation Battles Intensifying* (March 6, 2007), p. 2.

at all during Phase 1 and auctions continue to be limited going into Phase 2. No country has combined an auction with a reserve price to encourage development of new technology. The EC has limited the amount of auctioned allowances to 10% in Phase 2: a limit no country has chosen to meet. Efforts to expand auctions have met opposition from industry groups, but support from environmental groups and economists.

Currently, all U.S. cap-and-trade bills introduced have some provisions for auctions, although the amount involved is sometimes left to EPA discretion. Three bills, S. 317, S. 1766, and S. 2191 specify a schedule for the increased use of auctions with S. 317 allocating 100% of allowances by auction in 2036, S. 1766 allocating 66% by 2043, and S. 2191 allocating 73% by 2036. Funds would be used for a variety of purposes, including programs to encourage new technologies. None of the bills includes a reserve price on the auctions to create a price floor for new technology.

Like the situation in the ETS, most U.S. industry groups either oppose auctions outright or want them to be supplemental to a base free allocation. Given the experience with the ETS where the EC and individual governments have been unwilling or unable to move away from free allocation, the Congress may ultimately be asked to consider specifying any auction requirement if it wishes to incorporate market economics more fully into compliance decisions.

Flexibility and Price Volatility

Despite EU rhetoric during the Kyoto Protocol negotiations, it is moving into Phase 2 without a significant restriction on the use of CDM and JI credits. This embracing of project credits will significantly increase the flexibility facilities have in meeting their reduction targets. In addition, Phase 2 includes the use of banking to increase flexibility across time. Each of these market mechanisms is projected to reduce both the EU's Kyoto compliance costs and allowance price volatility. As a further defense against price volatility, the European emission exchanges are creating financial instruments, such as futures contracts and options, to permit entities to hedge against price changes.

Unfortunately, Phase 1 experience with the ETS does not provide much useful information on the value of market mechanisms or financial instruments in reducing costs or price volatility. The combination of poor emissions inventories, non-use of project credits, and time-limited allowances with effectively no banking resulted in extreme price volatility in Spring 2006, and virtually worthless allowances by mid-2007. The real test for the mechanisms employed by the ETS to create a stable allowance market is Phase 2.

Like the ETS, U.S. cap-and-trade proposals would employ a combination of devices to create a stable allowance market and encourage flexible, cost-effective compliance strategies by participating entities. All include banking. All include use of offsets, although some would place substantial restrictions on their use. One bill, S. 1766, incorporates a "safety valve" that would effectively place a ceiling on allowance prices. S. 2191 — America's Climate Security Act of 2007, which was reported by the Committee on Environment and Public Works on a 11 to 8 vote on

December 5, 2007 — would create a Carbon Market Efficiency Board to observe the allowance market and implement cost-relief measures if necessary. Some see this as a more flexible response with the potential for avoiding or mitigating the environmental impacts of a safety valve.

No current cap-and-trade proposal has specific provisions with respect to financial instruments or who would regulate such a market or its participants. One stand-alone bill, S. 2423, has been introduced in the 110th Congress to improve the transparency of emission allowance markets, and to address the potential for excessive speculation in those markets. Based on experience with the ETS, the potential for speculation and manipulation could extend beyond the emission markets. Analysis of ETS allowance prices during Phase 1 suggests the most important variables in determining allowance price changes were oil and natural gas price changes.[86] This apparent linkage between allowance price changes and price changes in two commodities markets raises the possibility of market manipulation, particularly with the inclusion of financial instruments such as options and futures contracts. Congress may ultimately be asked to consider whether the Securities and Exchange Commission or the Commodities Futures Trading Commission should have regulatory and oversight authority over such instruments.[87]

---

[86] Maria Mansanet-Bataller, Angel Pardo, and Enric Valor, "CO_2 Prices, Energy and Weather," 28 *The Energy Journal* 3 (2007), pp. 73-92.

[87] For a discussion of regulation of sulfur dioxide allowances as a commodity and implications for a greenhouse gas emissions market, see CRS Report RL34235, *Air Pollution as a Commodity: Regulation of the Sulfur Dioxide Allowance Market*, by Larry Parker and Mark Jickling.

CPSIA information can be obtained
at www.ICGtesting.com
Printed in the USA
BVHW060859100521
606948BV00012B/306